Copyrig

All rights reserved. No part of this book may be reproduced or used in any manner without written permission of the copyright owner except for the use of quotations in a book review. For more information, address: dyaniallenrnauthor@gmail.com

First paperback edition May 2021

Cover design by Jay Forth Ceed Anderson

ISBN 978-1-64775-352-8 (paperback)

Https://thernauthor.com/

https://consummateprofessionalsllc.com/

Dedication

This book is dedicated to my daughters, Kynidra Dyane and Aryana Janelle. You two were my first assignments as a caregiver. My love for you has been the motivation behind everything that I have tried to achieve. I am so proud of both of you!! I praise God for entrusting me with such beautiful and gifted daughters. Being your mother is my honor and privilege. I love you to infinity and beyond!!

Acknowledgments

To my Heavenly Father, I thank you for loving me and allowing me to serve your people. Thank you for every gift that you've given me. May they always be used to bring Glory to your name.

I'm thankful for every patient that has ever been entrusted to my care. I pray that the care you received from me impacted your life positively.

Lastly, to my fellow Caregivers. Whether you are caring for your own family or serving in the capacity of a private sitter, personal care attendant, Certified Nursing Assistant, Medical Assistant, Licensed Vocational Nurse, Registered Nurse, Nurse Practitioner, Nurse Anesthetist, Physician's Assistant, Occupational Therapist, Physical Therapist, Speech Therapist, Respiratory Therapist, Medical Doctor, Mother, Father, or whatever your specialized area may be. Thank you for all that you do!! Thank you for making a difference!!

Table of Contents

Prologue

Lord, I pour my troubles out to you.
Restore the peace that I once knew.

Distressed, distracted, and filled with shame
I feel unworthy to call on Your name

I remove self and seek your face
I'm trying, Lord. Cover me with your Grace.

When faced with temptations, help me make the right choice.
Quiet the chatter so that I may hear your voice.

Humbly I submit myself unto thee
For I know Your Truth will make me free

Safety is mine, if I rest in Your Will
So here am I Lord.
Yielded and Still

Day One

Humble Submission

Isaiah 55:8-9
(King James Version)

8 For my thoughts are not your thoughts, neither are your ways my ways, saith the Lord.
9 For as the heavens are higher than the earth, so are my ways higher than your ways, and my thoughts than your thoughts.

As Caregivers, we establish relationships with those who are entrusted to our care. We provide care with gentleness and compassion. We recognize that our ailing clients and their families are depending on us to be their advocate. We administer medications, render treatments, and perform procedures throughout the day hoping that we are making a difference. At the end of the day, we often question whether or not we've done enough.

Although we are knowledgeable and skilled in our profession, we are not deity. We are merely extensions of the Grace and Mercy of our

God. The suffering we encounter daily weighs heavily on our hearts and minds. We must humbly submit to the Sovereignty of an All Wise God. Tonight, lay it all at His feet.

Dear Heavenly Father, we bow in humble submission to your will. We pray that our words and deeds have been representative of your love. We know that your ways and thoughts are not as ours are. Help us to rest tonight knowing that You are God, and You alone. In You, all things are well. You are our conquering King and we adore You. Amen. Amen. Amen.

Day Two

God gets the Glory

1 Peter 4:10-11
As each one has received a special gift, employ it in serving one another as good stewards of the manifold grace of God. Whoever speaks, is to do so as one who is speaking the utterances of God; whoever serves is to do so as one who is serving by the strength which God supplies; so that in all things God may be glorified through Jesus Christ, to whom belongs the glory and dominion forever and ever. Amen.

As a young nurse, I was faced with many situations which helped to shape and mold my professional character. I cherish my experiences from my early nursing assignments. I recall working the night shift in a Long-Term Care Facility. There was a certain resident who despised people of color.

The elderly man's demeanor was vile and his words were venomous. He addressed me and the other African American Caregivers as 'Nigers'! No matter how much professional training you may have, it's extremely difficult to remain compassionate and empathetic towards someone who openly regards you with hate. Yet, every night I was polite and professional as I performed my duties.

One night, I entered this resident's room and observed him in obvious distress. He appeared to be having a heart attack. I instructed the Certified Nursing Assistant to call 911. As I provided care to this resident he reached out and grabbed my hand.

I will never forget the look of shear desperation and fear in his eyes. In that moment, he did not care about my skin color. I prayed aloud and was holding his hand as his earthly journey ended and his soul entered into eternity.

I will never know what his least thoughts were, but I'll forever feel grateful that God chose me to bring comfort during his dying moments. We have been chosen to serve. Our hearts and hands have been anointed to bring comfort and healing. As Caregivers, we must endeavor daily to Glorify God through our words and actions.

Lord, please help us to remain true to our faith, our vocation, and our calling. There are days when it seems that our efforts are in vain, but we know that every experience is working for our good. Give us temperance. Let our words and actions show forth the light of

your love. Please get the glory out of our lives. Amen.

Day Three

Respecting religious and cultural differences

"Be wise in the way you act toward outsiders; make the most of every opportunity. 6Let your conversation be always full of grace, seasoned with salt, so that you may know how to answer everyone," *Col. 4:5-6(NIV)*

I recall attending a function some years ago and being seated at a table with several people. As the conversation ensued, it was revealed that one of the men had religious views which differed from mine. I became determined to change his mind.

For the remainder of the evening, I passionately told him all of the reasons why he was a fool for believing as he did. I couldn't fathom why he couldn't feel and think as I did. At times, our voices were raised in anger. I had to make him know that Jesus is The Way.

Unfortunately, I didn't succeed. In fact, I failed miserably. The man was so offended by my delivery that he eventually left the table and sat somewhere else. My intentions were great, but my presentation was overbearing and rude.

As we provide care, we may encounter people of various spiritual practices. We must respect each individuals choices and lifestyles. How then, can we witness to them about our God?

Our compassionate care will introduce them to the Heart of God. Our gentle touch will acquaint then with the Hand of God. When we take time to listen and respond to their needs, God's love is displayed. Concern for their pain, discomfort, and their general well-being represents the Grace of God.

Endeavor daily to extend gentleness and benevolence through your care. God will provide opportunities for your to testify of His Goodness to you and thereby others will be introduced to your God. Let the Light of God's Love dispel the dark clouds of unbelief.

God, you such a Good and Perfect Father that I desire all to know you. I know that having you in my life has made all the difference and I want everyone to experience that joy that I have. Let the care I give be so demonstrative of your love that my clients will seek you. Help me to be alert to any opportunities to tell of Your Love. You are Good and Your Love us Everlasting. Amen.

Day Four

Dealing with burnout

Galatians 6:9 And let us not be weary in well doing: for in due season we shall reap, if we faint not. (KJV)

In 2018, I decided that I no longer wanted to continue in my career as a Director of Nursing. I felt as though my efforts were in vain. It didn't seem as though my work made a difference. I was a different type of tired. The kind of tired that's deep down inside. I hated going to work and decided to quit.

I took a couple of months to rest and reevaluate things. After a few weeks, I was miserable!!! God called me into this ministry of caregiving. When I walked away from His will, I couldn't find peace out contentment anywhere.

I sought direction through prayer and medication. I then realized that I was dealing with burnout. I was operating in self. I was relying on my knowledge and skills to get things done. I wasn't properly delegating tasks and was needlessly carrying the burden alone.

Caregivers endure an enormous amount of stress and strain. Don't allow the pressure of the profession cause you to miss out on the payout.

You are making a difference. You are appreciated. Your contributions matter. Stay the course.

Lord, help us to not give in not give up. Give us tenacity, patience and strength for this journey. When it seems that our work is in vain, remind us that the validation and compensation that we truly seek can only be rewarded by you. Lord we're leaning on and depending on you. In Jesus name, Amen.

Day Five

Laugh A Little

Job 8:21 - He will yet fill your mouth with laughter and your lips with shouts of joy

When was the last time you laughed until you cried? We often spend so much time dealing with the pressures of life that we forget to enjoy the moment. Life is meant to be lived!

Each moment should be cherished. Don't take for granted that there will be a next time. Live each day as if it were your last, it may be.
Sing that song you want to sing, even if it's off key. Dance a little, even if you have no rhythm. Wear that nice outfit, even if you have no where special to go. Love with all your might. Troubles and sorrows are plentiful but the Joy of the Lord is too.

So go ahead, throw your head back and laugh!! Laugh until your belly hurts. Laugh until the tears roll down your face. Laugh until you can't catch your breath. Rejoice! Be glad! Laugh!!

Thank you Father, for the gift of laughter. Thank you for the ability to feel emotions, to appreciate the highs and lows of life. Thank you for giving us this great joy that we have have inside. Help us to express this joy to others so that they too may experience it. You are a great God!! You are a Loving God. We exhaust exalt Your Name. There is none like You in all the earth. Be Glorified both now and forever, Amen!!

Day Six

Under Attack

"Be alert and of sober mind. Your enemy the devil prowls around like a roaring lion looking for someone to devour. Resist him, standing firm in the faith, because you know that the family of believers throughout the world is undergoing the same kind of sufferings."
1 Peter 5:8-9

Over the years, there have been many occasions when I felt as though I was surrounded by people on the job who's sole mission was to destroy me. The enemy comes to kill, steal and destroy. His mission is to create confusion and wreak havoc throughout the earth realm. He uses people as pawns and we all have fallen privy to the tricks of the enemy at one time or another.

During our season of attack, we must remember that we are in spiritual warfare. We focus on the person but lose sight of the bigger picture. Satan desires to separate us from the love of our Savior for eternity. When faced with great opposition, remember that we are children of the most high God. We're already more than conquerors. There is no plot of the enemy which our Lord has not already defeated!!! Walk in victory!!

Dear Father, being a caregiver is a stressful job. Often, we are under attack in the workplace. We are criticized, belittled and disrespected all while trying to give care to the sick. Help us to keep our eyes fixed on you. Help us to not be distracted by the ploys of Satan. We know that you will vindicate us. We pray that you will arise in every situation and the enemy be scattered. Thank you for being our Conquering King!!!! Amen.

Day Seven

Designer Originals

Ephesians 2:10 "For we are God's handiwork, created in Christ Jesus to do good works, which God prepared in advance for us to do."

We all have those times when we feel inadequate. We sometimes feel as though we're not good enough. In a world where we're constantly judged by the court of public opinion, it often seems as though we just don't measure up.

We are all Designer originals which have been crafted by God. We were created and predestined to serve those in need as Caregivers. You possess a uniqueness that only belongs to you.

Grow in the knowledge of God's word. Learn to walk in the path which has been set before you. Your steps have been preordained. Stand up. Stand out. Shine!!! Walk in your destiny!

Father God, thank you for lovingly creating each of us. Thank you for formulating a specific plan for our lives. We know that You made us in Your image. We are amazed by

your love for us. You have intricately woven together each detail of everything that gives us our identity. Help us learn to see ourselves as you see us. Shine through us and let Your Light illuminate our lives so that others may see You. Be glorified in our lives today. Amen!

Day Eight

Stay Focused

Psalm 46:10 , "Be still, and know that I am God; I will be exalted among the nations, I will be exalted in the earth." (NIV)

Healthcare is certainly what can be described as a cutthroat profession. The work Place seems to be inundated with people who display hidden agendas. They constantly display contemptible behavior through their malicious deeds. Often it seems as though the wicked flourish in their way while the righteous endure persecution.

We often lose sight of our mission as we are distracted by these seemingly personal attacks. We can become so focused on retribution that we lose our ability to render compassionate, empathetic care. Allow quality patient centered care to remain a priority and know that God will make all things right.

Heavenly Father, thank you for being concerned about every area of our lives. You know the number of hairs in our heads. We know that you see and know all things. Help us to rely on you to right the wrongs in our

lives. We pray that you would touch the hearts of those who come against us and give them a desire to know you in a real way. Help us to live lives that will bring Glory to Your name. Amen!

Day Nine

Faith and Family

1 Timothy 5:8 Anyone who does not provide for their relatives, and especially for their own household, has denied the faith and is worse than an unbeliever. (NIV)

Balancing work and home can be challenging. Trying to meet the demands of being a caregiver, we often drained of every at the end of the day. As a result, our families sometimes receive the 'short end of the stick'.

How do we find the right balance? We certainly love our spouses, children, parents, and siblings. However, we are conscientious and passionate concerning our professional responsibilities.

We must be mindful that our families are gifts from God. They are deserving of our affections and appreciation. Learning time management skills will aide us in maintaining an appropriate balance. When our homes are adequately provided for, we will be able to better serve the needs of our clients.

Lord, thank you for the gift of family. Forgive us for those times we've taken them for granted. Help us to cherish each day and every moment that we have with them. Please fill our hearts and homes with Your Joy, Peace, and Love. Help us to follow the example You have shown us. You are a Good, Good Father and we adore You. Amen.

Day Ten

Wrong Way!!

Proverbs 14:12 There is a way which seemeth right unto a man, but the end thereof are the ways of death. (KJV)

I love my car's turn by turn Navigation system. The system alerts you when you are approaching turns. One day, I was driving in a rural area. I was following the directives of the navigation system, or so I thought. Suddenly, I heard a message saying, "You have left the planned route. Directions will resume once you return to the route."

At this point, I became irritated. First of all, I followed the directions. (I was sure that I had). More importantly, how could the system dessert me in the middle of nowhere??? Then I heard the system ask, "Do you need updated directions?" I felt such a sense of relief that I hadn't been abandoned after all!!

In this world, we can often be mislead by adhering to societal standards. However, we must be ever mindful of God's word. When we stray from the right path, the Holy Spirit will speak to our hearts. He is always there to guide, we must only be willing to follow.

Father forgive us for those times when we stray. Help us to recognize your voice and your path. Give us more wisdom and courage from on high. Help us to always look to you. Please lead us as we seek to do your will. You are the Good Shepard and we belong to you. In the name of Jesus, Amen.

Day Eleven

God is in Control

John 14:27
Peace I leave with you; my peace I give you. I do not give to you as the world gives. Do not let your hearts be troubled and do not be afraid.

As a child, I learned a song entitled, "He's Got The Whole World In His Hand." In 2020, as the Coronavirus Pandemic created panic throughout the world, many of us participated in a social media challenge singing and declaring that God indeed has the whole world in His Hand. Healthcare workers were faced with insurmountable challenges. Staffing shortages were at an all time high. Personal Protective Equipment was scarce and hospitals were overwhelmed.

Coronavirus was like Goliath and Caregivers were like David. Coronavirus was like a universal plague that we would never eradicate. Day after day, Caregivers reported for duty to fight a battle which seemed impossible to win. There have been many days when we felt defeated and we witnessed patients, coworkers and family members succumb to the devastating virus.

Even now, Coronavirus continues to loom over us, a dark cloud of despair. Yet we continue to utilize the skills and knowledge that we have to bring healing and comfort to an ailing world. We know that our God is Greater than any problem that we will ever face. We trust in Jehovah Rapha, the God who heals.

Lord, sometimes we are distracted by the obstacles which lie before us. Help us to recognize that you are greater than any challenge we may face. During these times of uncertainty, reassure us that you are with us. We know that all power is in Your Hand and we're depending on you to see us through. Cover us with your Grace and protect us with your Mercy. In Jesus' Name, Amen.

Day Twelve

Give it to Jesus

Isaiah 41:10 (NIV) So do not fear, for I am with you; do not be dismayed, for I am your God. I will strengthen you and help you; I will uphold you with my righteous right hand.

Recently my daughter needed help finding a solution to a problem. She worked to solve it on her own for quite a while before she told me about the situation. She's my daughter and I love her, so Of course I stepped in and helped her.

I became very frustrated with her, asking why didn't you come to me at first? Why did you wait and make things worse before reaching out to me? The Holy Spirit immediately spoke into my spirit, "That's what God is asking you."

I begin to perform an introspective evaluation. I realized that I wrestle with many situations needlessly on a daily basis. God is patiently waiting for me to trust Him and turn it over to Him.

What are you fighting to fix today? God's word tells us that we can rely on Him. As you go through your day, confidently cast all of your cares upon Him and know that He'll work it out. He's dependable!

Father God, we thank you for being a Faithful Friend. Forgive us for those times when we walk in doubt and unbelief. We know that you love us and will withhold nothing good from us. Help us learn to fully rely on you. Help us to see you early. We know that in you, all things are made well. Thank you for your perfect love. In Jesus' name we pray, Amen!!!

Day Thirteen

Spot the Difference

Romans 12:2 (KJV) - And be not conformed to this world: but be ye transformed by the renewing of your mind, that ye may prove what [is] that good, and acceptable, and perfect, will of God

When I was younger, I used to enjoy reading the 'funny papers' section of the daily newspaper. There was always a section called Find the Difference. There would be two seemingly identical pictures side by side. However, there were slight differences in the two pictures. The challenge was being about to detect all of the differences. Two or three of the differences would be pretty obvious but the rest were usually difficult to find.

In today's society, finding the differences between the world and God's disciples has become increasingly challenging. We seem to have forgotten our identity and want to "fit in" with the crowd. We must remember that as followers of Christ we are called to stand out. It's often tempting to get caught up in what everyone else is doing but we must endeavor you do those things that are pleasing to our God.

Today, as you interact with patients, families and coworkers, ask yourself if others can find the difference between you and the nonbelievers. If your actions display a picture of obscured differences it's time to ask The Father to help you to be more like Him.

Holy One, help me to emulate you in my daily walk. My heart's desire is to live a life that's pleasing to you. Let my life do Glorify you that others will want to know you. Forgive me for my sins and cleanse me from anything that's not like you. I want to live for you. Amen.

Day Fourteen

Don't Give Up

Proverbs 24:16 (NIV) For though the righteous fall seven times, they rise again, but the wicked stumble when calamity strikes.

Have you ever tried to accomplish something and failed? No problem. You just try again, right? But what happens when you keep trying and you just can't seem to get it right?

Many times, we set goals both professional and personal, and it sometimes seems that the desired outcome is just out of reach. You've cried, you've prayed, and you've done everything that you know to do. Yet your aspirations are just beyond your grasp.

When God places a vision in your heart, He will certainly bring it to pass. Does that mean that there won't be obstacles? Demonic enmity will try to hinder anything that will bring God Glory. Let's be honest, often times SELF is our greatest opposition.

When we learn to seek God first and become sensitive to the directives of the Holy Spirit, we will experience triumph. Continue to pursue your dreams. Keep trusting and believing in what God has promised. It SHALL come to pass!!!

Lord, thank you for your Grace! Thank you for being a promise keeper! We may fall but we know that your strength will lift us again. Through you, we always win! In the name of He who Reigns Victorious, Jesus The Christ, we pray, Amen!!

Day Fifteen

Depression is Real

Psalm 30:11 (New International Version) You turned my wailing into dancing; you removed my sackcloth and clothed me with joy.

It's true that we never know what the next person is going through. We encounter people on a daily basis who put on a mask of happiness in public, yet cry silent tears when alone. Some wrestle daily with overwhelming feelings of sadness and despair.

If you are feeling isolated and as though no one cares, know that God is already loving you through your storm. In His infinite wisdom, God has equipped professional counselors in the earth realm. It's truly ok for Christians to seek counseling in addition to prayer and meditation.

Reach out to loved ones to support you through these dark days. God loves you and you matter to so many people. YOU ARE NOT ALONE!!

Oh Lord, our Lord, how excellent is Your name! You are our Conquering King and

there is truly None like You! Lord, there are days when we just don't feel like being strong anymore. The burdens of this world are heavy. We thank you for Jesus. We thank you that He walked this earthly road and understands our human frailties. God sometimes the tears freely fall and our hearts are filled with grief. Thank you for being a God who comforts us in it seasons of distress. Thank you for being our safe Haven. Your name is a strong tower, and therein the righteous are saved. Please be our strength during these troubled times. Thank you for your Holy Spirit interceding on our behalf when we don't know what to pray. Thank you for loving us. Comfort us, Oh God. Lift heavy burdens and ease aching hearts. We love you and adore you. In the matchless name of Jesus, Amen!!!!

Day Sixteen

The Solid Rock

Psalm 61:2 (New Living Translation)
From the ends of the earth, I cry to you for help when my heart is overwhelmed. Lead me to the towering rock of safety

Have you ever paid attention to a child's interaction with their parents? Children are quite interesting to observe. A child that's playing on the playground excitedly yells "Did you see me?" The child wants to share their triumphant moment with their caregiver. A little girl falls and scraped her knee. Immediately she seeks comfort from her mother. A little boy becomes afraid while walking in a crowd and grabs his father's hand, instantly feeling protected.

In a world that's ever shifting and changing, knowing that we have a solid place of security is reassuring. When the pressures of this world causes us to feel crushed and bruised, we can find refuge in God. He's faithful and forever the same. We can find comfort and protection in His Arms. His love is unwavering. How firm a foundation is our God!! Christ is our Solid Rock.

God, we are totally relying on you for guidance and strength. Thy will be done. Amen.

Day Seventeen

Words that Edify

1 Thessalonians 5:11 Therefore encourage one another and build up one another, just as you also are doing. (NIV)

Nursing is a profession that has been said to 'eat their young'. This phrase simply means that experienced nurses are often quite cruel and critical of novice nurses. What wasted opportunities!!!

Imagine if we all would take advantage of our interactions with others to impart words of wisdom. Words are powerful. We can cause irreparable damage to one who isn't as strong in the faith as we are.

Choose your words carefully. Edification of those we interact with daily will ultimately improve our work environments. Always use sensitivity when educating, being mindful that someone had to exercise patience with you. Allow your words to be extensions of the Grace which has been given to you through Christ Jesus.

Dear Father help us to use our words to encourage, edify, and educate others. Most of all, let our lives glorify you. Amen

Day Eighteen

Go to Sleep

Psalm 4:8 I will both lay me down in peace, and sleep: for thou, LORD, only makest me dwell in safety (KJV)

Caregivers often have trouble sleeping at night. We worry that the next shift won't follow through on the tasks that we didn't have time to complete. We feel guilty that we couldn't do more for our patient today. We carry a heavy load of guilt and feel bad that we didn't have more time to spend with our families and friends. We fret over what challenges we'll face tomorrow.

Tonight, let it go!!! Lie down knowing that God is truly in control of all things. When we've reached our limit, He steps in and displays His limitless power!! Give Him your worries and cares. Sleep.

Lord, thank you covering us with your grace throughout the day. Please allow your angels to watch over us tonight so that we may awake rejuvenated and ready to serve your people. In Jesus name, Amen.

Day Nineteen

Hope

Romans 15:13 May the God of hope fill you with all joy and peace as you trust in him, so that you may overflow with hope by the power of the Holy Spirit.

Have you ever faced a situation that seemed hopeless? You searched for solutions but there didn't seem to be any way out? We are surrounded by despair and desolate circumstances.

At times, it's difficult to remain optimistic within dismal conditions. Yet, we are not without hope. God is our eternal Hope. Draw near to Him and allow His joy and peace to fill you. Yes, there is Hope!!

Dear Father, sometimes our outlook seems dim. Help us to remember that there is nothing impossible for you. Our hope, confidence, and expectation is in you alone. You are our eternal hope.

Day Twenty

Go the Extra Mile

Luke 12:48b For everyone to whom much is given, from him much will be required; and to whom much has been committed, of him they will ask the more (New King James Version)

"Integrity is doing the right thing even if no one is watching." (Quote by C. S. Lewis)

God has generously gifted each of us. My gift may not look like yours, or Vice versa, but we each have unique talents and abilities. Healthcare is a ministry and we have been called to serve. Can you be trusted?

"Whenever you do a thing, act as if all the world are watching." (Quote by Thomas a' Kempis)

The world may not be watching, but our Lord sees all that we do. You have been entrusted with so much. Give your all every chance you get. You'll be amazed at how much richer your life will be.

Dear Heavenly Father, we thank you for choosing us to serve your people. We ask that you allow us to serve with hearts filled with love and compassion. We thank you for the strength and the desire to care for a world of hurting people. We pray that you will fill us with your love and that your light will shine through us. Thank you for keeping our minds focused on you. We love and adore you. In Jesus' name, Amen.

Day Twenty-One

The Perfect Gift

Romans 5:8 But God commendeth his love toward us, in that, while we were yet sinners, Christ died for us. (KJV)

Have you ever received an unexpected gift? Knowing that someone thought enough of you to give you a gift surely brightened your day!! There's an old saying that it's not the gift, but the thought that counts. I love giving gifts. (I also love receiving gifts!) I enjoy trying to find a special gift that will bring a smile to someone's face.

Our Heavenly Father gave us the gift that keeps giving. Jesus Christ made the ultimate sacrifice by dying on the cross for the redemption of our sins. He victoriously arose from the grave thereby forever freeing us from the bondage of sin. Thank you Holy Father for your Perfect Love!!

Thank you Lord for being our Risen Savior!! Because of your ultimate sacrifice, we are Forever freed from the bandage of sin. You are Holy and we adore you. Amen.

Day Twenty-Two

God Sees Your Tears

Psalm 56:8 You keep track of all my sorrows. You have collected all my tears in your bottle. You have recorded each one in your book. (New Living Translation)

So often our hearts are burdened with various problems which preoccupy our minds as we try to ease the pain and suffering of those in our care. I've heard people say "leave your problems at the door" but I've never truly agreed with it. Although we endeavor to give our clients our undivided attention, it's hard not to dwell on our personal situations.

We can be confident in knowing that our God is working on our behalf even while we are ministering to the needs of our clients. He knows or every concern and He cares. He will bear our every burdens, if only we'll give them over to Him.

Lord, please help us to know that you see all, you know all, and you can do anything but fail. Help us to totally and completely look to you for strength and direction. Earth has no

sorrow that Heaven cannot heal. We love and adore you.

Day Twenty-Three

We are Conquerors

Romans 8:37 Nay, in all these things we are more than conquerors through him that loved us.

Providing care for others is a formidable task. There are daily challenges which require professional proficiency and competency. There are times when we don't feel that we're properly prepared to perform the task at hand.

We can be assured in knowing that God will guide us through every situation. Stand tall and walk in confidence. You have been called to serve, adequately trained, and equipped to meet the needs of those entrusted in your care!

Dear God, some days I feel so defeated. Thank you for reminding me that I can't do anything alone, but in you I'm more than a conqueror. Thank you for being the God who is greater, stronger, and higher than any other. If you are for me, who can stand against me? You are the God who reigns. In you, I live, move and have my being. Amen.

Day Twenty-Four

It's All Good

Genesis 1:31 And God saw every thing that he had made, and, behold, it was very good. And the evening and the morning were the sixth day. (KJV)

Have you ever taken time to evaluate your life and just tell God thank you? We complain so much about the things we don't have that we overlook the abundance of blessings all around us. Our God created this wonderful world and everything in it in just six days!!!

Man may have failed in stewardship but the world God gave us is astoundingly beautiful! What an awesome God we serve!!! Take time out today to enjoy and appreciate all that God created, but most importantly remember to express sincere praise and agitation to God, the Creator of all things!

Lord, we thank you for your manifold blessings. Father we ask your forgiveness for all of the times when we walk in doubt and fear. We know that you are Lord of all Able to

do exceeding, above all that we can ask or think. This life is hard. This world is filled with mean and hateful people. We know that everything you created is good. Help us to see the good in every situation. Help us to put our trust and expectation in you and you alone. You are sovereign and all power belongs to you. Thank you for being our sustainer, comforter, and refuge. You are our joy, and therein lies our strength! Thank you for being God!

Day Twenty-Five

He knows

Job 42:2 "I know that you can do all things, and that no purpose of yours can be thwarted."

About twenty years ago, the movie Boyz In The Hood was released. This movie movie was set in a crime infested and impoverished neighborhood. One of the characters, Doughboy, was saddened and frustrated by the conditions. He made a statement, concerning the government, that " Either they don't know, don't show, or don't care about what's going on in the hood."

Many times it seems as though no one cares. Does God see? Does He hear? How can He allow these things to happen? Job was a perfect and upright man, yet God allowed him to be tested. We often ask, "Why me?" But do we ever ask ourselves, "Why not me?"

Although troubles and tragedies are all around us, God is always in control. He will not leave us. In the midst of every trial, know that He is there to comfort, strengthen, and keep us.

Sovereign God, we come this morning acknowledging that you are the only true and living God. We confess our sins to you and ask that you would forgive us. Lord, the current condition of this world is alarming but we know that you have not given us a spirit of fear. Help us to rely on you, knowing that the safest place in the whole world is in your will. Give us insight, give us strength, and enable us to care for our patients with compassion. We know that our only hope is in you and we trust you. In Jesus name, Amen!!!

Day Twenty-Six

When I Am Afraid

Psalm 56:3 What time I am afraid, I will put my trust in thee. (American Standard Version)

We're living in scary times!!! The daily news is filled with destruction, violence and despair. The world wide pandemic of Coronavirus has caused even the strongest of us to be afraid. How can we continue to minister to the needs of the people while we are fearing for our safety?
We know that we've been called to serve, yet we want to remain safe while keeping our loved ones safe. As we are surrounded by sickness and grief, we must rely on our All Powerful God to protect us from all hurt harm and danger. God is out refuge and we can find safety in Him!

All knowing and all powerful God, we come to you during this time of uncertainty relying on you to guide us. Although this epidemic is new to us, we know that you are omnipotent, omnipresent, and omniscient! We thank you for being a loving and merciful God. We thank

you for keeping us, even in the midst of this world's chaos.
We may not know everything about COVID-19, but we know you to be Jehovah-Rapha the Lord who heals; you're Jehovah-Nissi the Lord our banner; you're Jehovah-Shalom the Lord our peace; Jehovah-Jireh The Lord will provide!!! You are El Shaddai, God Almighty. You are Elohim, Creator, Mighty and a Strong!
Your name is a strong tower, the righteous can take refuge in you. You have been our dwelling place for generations. You've never failed us and we are confident that you will sustain us, even now.
Please God, hear our cries and comfort, strengthen, and keep us.
Now unto the King, Eternal, Immortal, Invisible, the ONLY God, be honor and glory for ever and ever
AMEN! AMEN! AMEN!

Day Twenty-Seven

Access Granted

Matthew 27: 51 And, behold, the veil of the temple was rent in twain from the top to the bottom; and the earth did quake, and the rocks rent (King James Version)

The past few years have been filled with a series of unprecedented events. Just when you think things can't get any worse, they do. Every one has turned their own way. Even in many of our churches, popular opinion has replaced God's Holy Word!!! This world is filled with turmoil and at times we feel oppressed and hopeless.

During these turbulent times, we can be reassured in the knowledge that our God is a very present help in the time trouble!! He's already conquered sin and death, when He victoriously arose from the grave. We have been granted direct access to our Heavenly Father, and He will help us as we sojourn through this world.

Lord, we thank you for the privilege of prayer. Thank you hearing and answering our cries.

Have mercy on us, even now. We as a people have failed to reference you as Lord in our daily walks and we repent. In this hour, there is no help, there is no answer other than you. You are sovereign and all power belongs to you. Oh Lord, have mercy upon us according to your loving kindness. Keep us in the palm of your righteous hand and save us!! Lord, our confidence is in you alone.

Now unto him that is able to keep you from falling, and to present you faultless before the presence of his glory with exceeding joy. To the only wise God our Saviour, be glory and majesty, dominion and power, both now and ever. Amen. (Jude 1:24-25, KJV)

Day Twenty-Eight

Chaos

John 14:27 Peace I leave with you; my peace I give you. I do not give to you as the world gives. Do not let your hearts be troubled and do not be afraid.

CHAOS

Calamities *and* ***Havoc*** *are all around us. We are filled with* ***apprehensions*** *and unrest.*
Throughout the land, there is social unrest and ***ostracism*** *of those who would walk in the plain path.* ***Seditious*** *acts of public figures have created strife and sorrow. We are troubled and afraid.*

CALM

Yet, we are confident and **comforted**!!! We have the Blessed **Assurance** of knowing that the **Lord of Lords** loves us. God, in His **Majesty**, will make all things well.

Heavenly Father we need you. All around us, there is sickness, grieve, and despair. Help us to remember that you are still God and you

are still in control. You are the only hope we have, a very present help in the time if trouble. Help us to keep our eyes fixed on the problem solver. Forgive us for turning away from you, for lusting after the things of this world. Renew in us a right spirit. Restore unto us the joy of our salvation. Refresh us with your love. As we remember your sacrifice during this week, we are reminded that you've already conquered sin and death. You are Sovereign, Supreme, and Victorious God!!! Nothing is too hard for you. Nothing is beyond your control. You made us and you know all about us. You've truly got the whole world in your hand. Please keep us and oh merciful God, please save us!!! Give us the strength we need to care for your people. Be our buffer and shield. Lord, we trust you.
In Jesus name, Amen!!!! □□□□□□

Day Twenty-Nine

Self-Care

Mark 6:31 (New Living Translation)
Then Jesus said, "Let's go off by ourselves to a quiet place and rest awhile." He said this because there were so many people coming and going that Jesus and his apostles didn't even have time to eat.

A caregiver's days are often hectic and filled with fulfilling the needs of those who have been intruded to their care. While focusing on the needs of others, the caregiver often neglects self. Ignoring personal needs and desires often becomes 'the norm' for many caregivers.

Learning to take care of one's self can be accompanied by feelings of guilt. The caregiver has engaged in the act of altruism for so long that it seems selfish to indulge in our personal care. Eleanor Brown best stated, "Self-care if not selfish. You cannot serve from an empty vessel."

Promote making self a priority. When we are refreshed, restored, and rejuvenated we are able to share our best selves with our clients and families. So go ahead, take your lunch break, go for that walk, pamper yourselves. Do those things that are necessary to replenish and care for self. Most importantly, make time daily to commune with God the Father. Start today!!

Lord help us to remember that we are valuable and precious in your sight. Help us to care for ourselves so that we may be of greater service to your people and do greater works for you. In Jesus' name, Amen!

Day Thirty

Free Indeed!

2 Corinthians 3:17 Now the Lord is the Spirit; and where the Spirit of the Lord *is*, there *is* liberty.

I love driving on the open highway. There's something about being out on the roadways that eases my anxieties. I feel uninhibited by the stressors of life and I'm able to have clarity of thoughts. Simply put, I feel free.

Our Lord and Savior came into this world to free of us from the eternal bondage of sin. He was born of a virgin, lived a sinless life, was crucified, died on a cross, and was buried in a borrowed tomb. The amazing part is the He arose from the grave thereby forever granting us true liberty!!!!

As disciples of Christ, we are free and free indeed!!!! God has given us the victory through Christ Jesus. We are no longer bound by the temporary trials of this world. We have confidence in knowing that He has prepared us an eternal Home in Heaven with Him!!

Choose to make Him your Lord today and you too can be FREE INDEED!!!

Lord we thank you for loving us so much. We thank you for enduring pain and suffering on our behalf. Most of all we thank you for Redeeming us with your precious blood. Please Hide us from the enemy under your wing of protection. Hold us with your Righteous Right Hand and keep us close to you. We thank you for your joy and peace and was sojourn through this life. Most of all, we praise you for Freeing us from shame and guilt! You've paid the ultimate price to settle our debt and we are grateful. You are an Awesome God. You are Holy and You are Faithful. Lead us and Guide us through these earthly trials. When this life is over, please Master, call us, receive us, and reward us. Most of all, we want to hear You say, (Mathew 25:23) 'Well *done,* good and faithful servant; you have been faithful over a few things, I will make you ruler over many things. Enter into the joy of your lord.' Amen! Amen! Amen!

Made in the USA
Columbia, SC
17 June 2024

36610656R00037